Everything That Has Fish, Is Now Vegan

Don't Give Up Your Favorite Recipes Just Because It Has Fish

Riki Berko

First Edition 2015

ISBN-13: 978-1507630631
ISBN-10: 1507630638

Free E-books Club:

I would like to give you FREE GIFT for your child and a full access to my VIP club in which you receive FREE children's e-books once they are published:

Receive Free E-books Here:
http://bit.ly/150k24J

I do this simply because I want my readers to get a lot of value, reach their maximum potential and have a better life. Be the change you want to see in the world!

TABLE of CONTENTS

Sushi

For Kids

DRESSINGS and SAUCES

LIST of INGREDIENTS

INDEX, alphabetical

Recommended Books

INTRODUCTION

How many times have you felt a craving for a certain recipe that you used to eat before you have gone vegan and had to "give it up"? or how many times have you heard people say: "Oh, I could never go vegan. I like X so much, I can't give it up". Well there is no need to give up on your favorite recipes just because they have cheese in them. Now you can make all of them in their vegan version and this book is going to show you how. All you have to do is be a little creative.

"Creativity is seeing what everyone else has seen, and thinking what no one else has thought."
-Einstein-

So you've decided to exclude animal products. Do you feel like you have "dietary restrictions"? Need to lose 15 pounds for your wedding? Or maybe you just like trying new things. You might be wading gingerly into this lifestyle from vegetarianism, or instead jumping in as a "cold turkey" convert—no pun intended.

Whatever your reason for choosing to eat vegan, throughout this book you'll find plenty of tips, tricks, and treats for cooking vegan dishes that originally included fish and seafood.

I encourage sticking to the original recipes as you first make them but feel free to add, substitute, and cut ingredients which don't suit your time or budget. Cooking should be fun and fulfilling! So grab an apron, turn on the tunes, and I'll meet you at the cutting board…

"Stay committed to your decisions, but stay flexible in your approach."
— Tom Robbins

THE BASICS

Types of Fish

We are going to make some alternative vegan fish recipes to use as basic ingredients for the recipes.

FISH OR SEAFOOD	VEGAN FISH
Salmon	Vegan Fish Filet or Vegan Salmon spread
Tuna	Vegan Tuna
Trout, Cod, or Halibut	Vegan Fish Filet
Shrimp	Vegan Shrimp
Crab	Vegan Crab

Types of Edible Seaweed

Arame
Badderlocks
Bladderwrack
Carola
Carrageen moss
Channelled wrack
Chlorella
Cochayuyo
Dulse
Ecklonia cava
Eucheuma
Eucheuma spinosum
Eucheuma cottonii
Gutweed
Gelidiella
Graciraria
Gracilaria edulis
Gracilaria corticata
Hijiki or Hiziki
Hiromi
Hypnea

Irish moss
Kombu
Laver
Limu Kala
Mozuku
Nori
Oarweed
Ogonori
Sugar kelp
Sea grapes or green caviar
Sargassum
Sargassum cinetum
Sargassum vulgare
Sargassum swartzii
Sargassum myriocysum
Sea lettuce
Spiral wrack
Spirulina
Thongweed
Wakame

How to Make Vegan Fish and Seafood

VEGAN FISH FILET

This recipe works for general fish substitution. You can apply any glaze or marinade, and prepare it baked, steamed, fried, or grilled.

Ingredients:

Fish:
2 lbs yuba *
3 tsp white sugar
6 tsp vegetarian bouillon powder
Salt, to taste
Kelp granules, to taste
6 Tbsp arrowroot powder

1 ½ Tbsp sesame oil
Nori sheets

Glue:
2 Tbsp arrowroot powder
2 Tbsp warm water

Method:

1) Chop the yuba into small flakes, squeezing out any extra moisture.
2) Transfer the yuba to a large bowl and add sugar, bouillon powder, salt, kelp granules, arrowroot powder, and sesame oil. Mix well.
3) Mix the glue.
4) *To assemble the fish*: Lay a nori sheet onto a cutting board. Brush the sheet with the glue. Spoon about 1 cup of the 'fish' mixture on the bottom half of the nori sheet, leaving an extra ½" on the vacant side. Wet fingers and press the mixture firm. Fold the remaining sheet over the mound, sealing the ½" overlap with glue like an envelope. Your ends should be exposed.
5) Repeat the process with remaining nori sheets until all the mixture is used.
6) Steam the filet for 20-25 minutes.

   **NOTE: Yuba is also called tofu skin, so you may need to ask for it under multiple names at your local Asian market.

VEGAN SALMON SPREAD

Use this spread on crackers or as a dip for vegetables. The parsley helps freshen breath, despite the fishy flavor.

Ingredients:

1 can chickpeas, drained
1 package smoked tofu
1 Tbsp almond butter
1 Tbsp tahini

1/2 t tsp Spanish Smoked Paprika
1 Tbsp lime juice
1 Tbsp chopped fresh parsley

Method:

1) Using a food processor combine all the ingredients, adjusting spices to personal taste.
2) Blend until smooth.

VEGAN TUNA

This tuna is a great substitute for cold salads and sandwiches. Here is the base recipe, but feel free to play around with added flavors and textures.

Ingredients:

1/3 cup sunflower seeds, soaked
1/4 cup mung bean sprouts
3 Tbsp almond butter
1 Tbsp kelp flakes

1 tsp nama shoyu
1/2 cup yellow onion
2 celery stalks
Salt, to taste

Method:

3) Using a food processor combine sunflower seeds, mung bean sprouts, almond butter, kelp powder*, nama shoyu*, and salt*. Blend until mixture reaches a smooth paste.
4) Add the onion and celery, pulsing until blended but still chunky.

*NOTE: Increase the "fishy" flavor by adding more kelp, nama shoyu, and salt.

VEGAN SHRIMP

Whether you boil or fry these shrimp dumplings, they're tasty in both appetizers and pastas alike!

Ingredients:

Shrimp:
1 cup gluten flour
1 tsp garlic powder
1 tsp paprika
1/2 cup sweet potato puree (fresh or jarred)
1+ Tbsp coconut oil, melted

Broth:
8 cups water
Salt, to taste
1-2 Tbsp dulse seaweed*

Method:
1) Sift together the gluten flour, garlic powder, and paprika.
2) In another bowl, combine the sweet potato puree and the oil.
3) Mix the dry ingredients into the wet, and knead by hand until a smooth dough forms, about 3 minutes.
4) Roll the dough to ½" thickness and slice into strips.
5) *To boil the shrimp*: In a medium saucepan, combine water, salt and seaweed to make a broth. Stir well, and bring to a boil. Twist the strips then bring the ends together. Pinch to close. Drop the dough into the broth, and cook about 10 minutes, or until shrimp is floating to top and cooked through. **
6) Remove the shrimp, immediately placing on a paper towel to drain. Fry immediately.
7) *To fry the shrimp*: In a skillet, melt 3 Tbsp coconut oil over medium heat. Add the shrimp and fry, stirring occasionally, for 5-8 minutes.
8) Turn the shrimp out on a plate, and serve immediately.

   *NOTE: There are many different kinds of seaweed that would work, depending on personal tastes. See the complete list in THE BASICS.

   ** NOTE: Depending on the size of your pot, a typical batch of shrimp should consist of 6-10 dough pieces. Do not crowd.

VEGAN CRAB

Use this faux crab meat for crab cakes and sushi rolls.

Ingredients:

1 package tempeh or tofu
3 Tbsp tamari
4 oz vegan cream cheese

Kelp flakes, to taste
Salt, to taste
1/3 cup slivered almonds, chopped finely

Method:
1) Squeeze as much liquid from the tofu as possible.
2) Mince the tofu into 1/8" squares.
3) In a separate bowl mix tamari, cream cheese, kelp flakes, salt, and almonds. Let stand 10 minutes.
4) Add the sauce to the tofu. Mix well.

BREAKFAST

BAGELS and LOX

Pair this classic with a fresh cup of coffee, a good book, and a misty morning.

Ingredients:

Vegan Salmon spread
I pack of bagels, halved*
Vegan Cream Cheese
Fresh dill

Capers
Tomato, thinly sliced
Red onion, diced
Cracked black pepper, to taste

Assembly:
1) Spread cream cheese on the bagel half.
2) Follow with the Vegan Salmon spread.
3) Sprinkle a pinch of dill atop the spread.
4) Add capers, tomato, and onion to taste.
5) Finish with pepper.

*NOTE: Most bagels should be Vegan, as basic bread dough is made from flour, water, salt, and yeast. But just in case, read your ingredients!

FISHERMAN's HASH

Perfect for Sunday Brunches, Holiday Breakfasts, or Rainy Days.

Ingredients:

3 Tbsp. flax meal
1 Tbsp. warm water
2 cups *vegan fish filet*, flaked
1 cup golden potatoes (diced, boiled, cooled)*
1 cup sweet potatoes (diced, boiled, cooled)*

1 cup kale, shredded
1 red bell pepper, diced
1 tablespoon red onion, minced
Salt and pepper, taste
3 Tbsp coconut oil

Method:
1) In a bowl, combine the flax meal and water. Stir well. Let sit 5-10 minutes until the water becomes slimy.
2) In a separate bowl combine fish, potatoes, kale, bell pepper, salt, and pepper.
3) Add the flax mixture. Mix well.
4) In a large skillet, melt the coconut oil over medium high heat.
5) Add the entire mixture to the skillet, stirring frequently until cooked through.

* NOTE: Cook your potatoes until *al dente*, or just tender. Drain potatoes and cool immediately under cold running water.

"Today, more than ever before, life must be characterized by a sense of Universal responsibility, not only nation to nation and human to human, but also human to other forms of life."
– Dalai Lama

SPICY SALMON SCRAMBLE

Try tofu or tempeh for an egg-cellent texture choice. Enjoy the scramble with avocado and tomato on toast, or wrapped in a tortilla with hot sauce.

Ingredients:

3 Tbsp *vegan salmon spread*
2 Tbsp coconut oil
1/2 yellow onion, diced
3 cloves garlic, minced
1 tsp nama shoyu
1 package tofu, cut into 1" cubes
1/2 green bell pepper
1/2 cup brussel sprouts, steamed and diced

3/4 cup mushrooms, sliced
3 scallions, sliced
12 grape tomatoes, sliced
1/2 tsp ginger , ground
1/2 tsp chili powder
1/4 tsp cayenne pepper
1/2 tsp Spanish smoked paprika
Salt and Pepper, to taste

Method:

1) In a skillet over medium heat, melt the oil. Add onions and garlic, cooking until fragrant.
2) Add the nama shoyu, tofu, and Vegan Salmon spread, cooking on medium-low heat.
3) Add the vegetables and spices. Cook until soft.

No man is an island,
Entire of itself,
Every man is a piece of the continent,
A part of the main.
If a clod be washed away by the sea,
Europe is the less.
As well as if a promontory were.
As well as if a manor of thy friend's
Or of thine own were:
Any man's death diminishes me,
Because I am involved in mankind,
And therefore never send to know for whom the bell tolls;
It tolls for thee.

- John Donne

CRAB QUICHE

Enjoy this Sunday brunch dish by the sea or by the fireplace. It tastes delicious warm or cold!

Ingredients:

To Prepare:
1 pastry crust
1 ¼ cup cauliflower, chopped
2 teaspoons coconut oil, melted
1/4 teaspoon salt
1 yellow onion, finely sliced
1 red bell pepper, sliced
1 green bell pepper, sliced

For the quiche mixture:
1 cup chickpea flour
2 ½ cups water
1 vegetable bouillon cube
1/2 tsp sage
1/2 tsp turmeric, ground
3 Tbsp nutritional yeast
2 cups *vegan crab*
Salt, to taste

Method:

1) Preheat the oven to 400°F.
2) *To prepare the cauliflower*: Place the cauliflower in a bowl with 1 teaspoon oil and 1/4 teaspoon salt. Coat well. Place on a lined baking sheet and roast 15-20 minutes until softened and slightly charred. Remove and let cool.
3) *To prepare the onions and peppers*: In another bowl, add the rest of the oil to a skillet and caramelize the onions, with a pinch of salt, for 5 minutes on low heat. Add the bell peppers and cook until soft.
4) *To prepare the crust*: Oil and flour the quiche dish. Place the pastry in the dish, pricking the bottom with a fork. Bake for 15 minutes. Remove from the oven and let cool.
5) *To prepare the filling*: In a bowl add the flour and 1 cup water. Whisk together and let sit. In a saucepan, add the remaining water, bouillon cube, sage, turmeric, nutritional yeast, and salt. Bring to a boil. Slowly pour in the flour mixture and stir continuously. Turn the heat to low and continue to stir continuously for 2-3 minutes until the mixture becomes thick and glossy. Add in the cauliflower, vegetables, and crab mixture. Stir well.
6) Pour into the prepared crust, leveling with a spatula.
7) Cook for 20-25 minutes, or until springy to the touch.

"Our greatest responsibility is to be good ancestors"
– Jonas Salk

SOUPS

FISH BROTH

Use this broth as a base for your seafood soups, chowders, and stews.

Ingredients:

1/2 cups shredded wakame
2 cups filtered water
2 large garlic cloves, crushed
1 tsp whole peppercorns

1/3 cup shitake mushrooms
1 Tbsp nama shoyu
Salt, to taste

Method:

1) Combine wakame, water, garlic, and peppercorns in a large sauce pan. Bring to a boil.
2) Lower heat and simmer about 20-25 minutes. Strain the solids, and return the liquid back to the pot.
3) Add soy sauce. Bring liquids back to a boil. Cook until mixture is reduced by one-half and very salty.

Health is a state of complete physical, mental and social well-being, and not merely the absence of disease or infirmity.
- World Health Organization, 1948

MISO SOUP

Miso soup is a traditional Japanese soup well-known around the world. It's quick and easy to cook with lots of salt, making it ideal for sore throats and chilly mornings.

Ingredients:

4 cups *Fish Broth*

3 Tbsp miso paste

1 package tofu, cubed

12 scallions, chopped

Method:

1) In a saucepan, bring the broth to a boil. Gradually whisk in the miso paste.
2) Add the tofu and simmer 3-5 minutes.
3) Add the scallions before serving.

CLAM CHOWDER

You don't need to travel to New England to try this delicious chowder! Serve it with oyster crackers or vegan cornbread for a winter treat.

Ingredients:

2 red potatos, diced
3 Tbsp kelp flakes
1 Tbsp coconut oil
1 yellow onion, diced
2 cloves garlic, minced
2 stalks celery, thinly sliced
2 carrots, sliced
1 Tbsp dried thyme
2 bay leaves

3 Tsp dulse flakes
½ cup dry white wine
½ cup sherry
1/3 cup coconut oil
1/3 cup gluten flour
1 ½ cup shitake mushrooms, chopped
1 cup cauliflower, steamed and mashed
Pinch nutmeg, freshly grated
Parsley

Method:

1) In a saucepan, combine the kelp with 1 cup water. Let sit for 30 min. Bring to a slow boil, then take off heat. Let cool. Strain and keep the liquid.
2) In a pot, cover the potatoes with water and bring to a boil. Boil until tender, but firm. Drain.
3) In a medium saucepan, sauté onion in 1Tbsp oil until soft.
4) Add the garlic, celery, and carrots and sauté briefly.
5) Add thyme and dulce.
6) Add white wine and sherry, and the bay leaves. Turn to low heat.
7) *To make the roux:* In a large pot, melt 1/3 cup oil on low heat. Add the flour, and whisk constantly for a few minutes—taking care not to burn—until smooth.
8) Add the onion and sherry mix from your saucepan to the roux. Stir well.
9) Add the kelp liquid and bring to a boil, stirring constantly.
10) Reduce heat, add the mushrooms and cauliflower. Simmer for 5 minutes, or until mushrooms are springy.
11) Garnish with nutmeg and parsley.

There's lots of people in this world who spend so much time watching their health that they haven't the time to enjoy it.
- Josh Billings

THAI COCONUT SOUP with SHRIMP

This soup can be made sweet or savory. If you want a fishier flavor, substitute *Fish Broth* for the vegetable broth.

Ingredients:

Vegan shrimp
3 cloves garlic, minced
1/2 red onion, sliced
1 carrot, sliced thin
1 cup shiitake mushrooms, sliced
1 Tbsp olive oil
1 Green Thai pepper, minced

1 ½ cups vegetable broth
1 can coconut milk
5 slices ginger
5 slices lemongrass
Juice from one lime
1 package tofu, chopped into 1-inch cubes
2 Tbsp chopped fresh cilantro

Method:

1) In a large pot, sauté the garlic, onion, carrot, and mushrooms in oil until fragrant.
2) Reduce heat to low and add the pepper, vegetable broth, coconut milk, ginger, lemongrass, lime juice, and tofu.
3) Simmer for 15 minutes.
4) Garnish with shrimp and cilantro.

SALADS

PESTO TUNA SALAD

Buying ready-made pesto decreases the preparation work, but you can easily make your own with fresh basil from the garden.

Ingredients:

1 cup *vegan tuna*
6 Tbsp Pesto
1 cup vegan pasta, cooked and cooled
½ cup walnuts, toasted and chopped
1 cup romaine lettuce, chopped

Method:

1) In a large bowl, combine all the ingredients, mixing well.
2) Spread the salad over bread, or eat with crackers.

Until one has loved an animal, a part of one's soul remains unawakened.
- Anatole France

CESAR SALAD

Croutons make this salad traditional, but apples and celery give it a sweet edge like its cousin, the Waldorf.

Ingredients:

1 cup romaine lettuce, chopped
1/3 cup apples, chopped
1/3 cup celery, chopped
¼ cup vegan cheese

¼ cup sliced almonds, toasted
Vegan croutons to taste
Cesar Dressing

Method:

1) In a large bowl, combine the lettuce, apples, celery, cheese, almonds, and croutons.
2) Add the dressing, tossing until entire salad is covered. Serve immediately.

Our task must be to free ourselves... by widening our circle of compassion to embrace all living creatures and the whole of nature and its beauty.
- Albert Einstein

VEGAN SEAFOOD POTATO SALAD

This mock seafood salad is very filling with the potatoes. It makes a great seaside picnic lunch or an easy surprise for a hard-working spouse.

Ingredients:

1 cup *vegan crab*
1 cup *vegan shrimp*, chopped
3 red potatoes, diced and boiled
1/2 cup celery, chopped
1/2 cup carrots, shredded
1/2 cup cauliflower, lightly steamed
1/3 cup shallots, minced 2

2 cloves garlic, minced
2 Tbsp sweet relish
1 Tbsp yellow mustard
3/4 to 1 cup vegan mayonnaise
Salt and pepper, to taste
2 cups watercress
1 tsp paprika

Method:

1) In a large bowl, mix the crab, shrimp, potatoes, celery, carrots, and cauliflower.
2) In another bowl, mix the shallots, garlic, relish, mustard, mayonnaise, salt and pepper.
3) Combine the mustard mixture with the vegetable-fish mixture.
4) Serve the salad atop watercress. Sprinkle finished salad with paprika.

APPETIZERS

CEVICHE

Celebrate the Central and South American heritage with this classic summer party-food.

Ingredients:

3 cups *vegan shrimp*, chopped
1 cup lime juice
1/2 cup lemon juice
1/3 cup white onion, diced
1/3 cup purple onion
1 cup cucumber

1 cup tomato, diced
1 Jalapeño, diced
1 Serrano chili, diced
1 bunch cilantro, chopped
4 Tbsp olive oil
Salt and pepper, to taste

Method:

1) In a large bowl, mix the shrimp and citrus juices. Let sit 1 hour.
2) In another bowl, mix the rest of the ingredients.
3) Add the marinated shrimp to the vegetable mixture and season to taste.
4) Serve immediately.

The greatness of a nation and its moral progress can be judged by the
way its animals are treated.
-Mohandas Gandhi

VEGAN CRAB CHEESE WONTONS

Wontons pair well with sweet and sour sauce, but also consider a teriyaki dip or vegan ranch dressing.

Ingredients:

1 package vegan cream cheese
1 cup crab meat
1/2 cup scallions, chopped
1 Tbsp Tamari

1 tsp garlic powder
Coconut or peanut oil, for frying
Wonton wrappers

Method:

1) In a small pot, heat 1" of oil.
2) Squeeze the crabmeat in cheesecloth or against a sieve to drain as much liquid as possible.
3) In large bowl combine the cream cheese, crabmeat, green onions, tamari and powder. Mix well.
4) Spoon 1 tsp of the crab mixture into a wrapper. Pinch the opposite corners together, making a little package.
5) Repeat until all the crab mixture is used.
6) Carefully drop the packages into the oil. Depending on the size of your pot, fry 5-8 wontons at a time. Do not crowd.
7) Fry the wontons until golden, about 2-3 minutes. Drain on a paper towel.

VEGAN SALMON ROSEMARY PATTIES

Try serving these patties over a spinach salad with a light drizzle of white wine vinaigrette.

Ingredients:

1 cup *vegan salmon spread*
1/2 cup sweet potato purée
1/2 cup quinoa
1 cup gluten flour
2 Tbsp fresh rosemary, chopped

3 cloves garlic, minced
1 Tbsp parsley, chopped
Coconut oil, for frying
Toasted pine nuts

Method:

1) In a skillet, heat 3 Tbsp of oil.
2) In a large bowl combine the salmon, purée, 3/4 cup of flour, rosary, garlic, and parsley. Mix well.
3) Place the remaining 1/4 cup of flour on a plate.
4) Form the salmon mixture into 2" balls and press flat. Coat the rounds in flour. So this for the remaining mixture.
5) Carefully place the rounds in the oil, frying on each side for 2-3 minutes or until golden.
6) Garnish the patties with pine nuts.

"Nothing strengthens the judgment and quickens the
conscience like individual responsibility."
- Elizabeth Cady Stanton

VEGAN TUNA MELTS

Serve the melts open faced, or make sandwiches to dip in catsup or tomato soup!

Ingredients:

3/4 cup *vegan tuna*
2 slices white onion
1 Tbsp parsley, chopped

4 slices vegan cheese
2 slices whole wheat or sourdough bread, toasted

Method:

1) To assemble:
2) Spread tuna over bread slices. Top with white onion and parsley. Layer cheese on top.
3) If making an open face: place bread under a broiler for 3-5 minutes or until cheese is melted.
4) If making a sandwich, finish with a top slice of bread and grill on a panini maker, or press down with a pan.

CRAB CAKES

These cakes fry best after being squeezed. Watch for splattering oil on clothes and skin. Serve atop rice, quinoa, or vegan tartar sauce. Better yet, make Edamame hummus!

Ingredients:

1 cup *vegan crab*, divided into thirds
4 Tbsp flour
Coconut Oil

Method:

1) In a skillet over medium heat melt 3 Tbsp coconut oil.
2) Pour the flour into a flat plate.
3) *To make the cakes:* Take 1/3 of the crab and squeeze it in cheesecloth or against a small sieve. Form the meat into a ball and press flat. Coat each side with flour.
4) Carefully drop the cakes into the oil and fry for 2 minutes on each side, or until golden.
5) Repeat with the remaining two thirds.

FISH KEBABS

These kebabs look very exotic served over black rice, though white will taste good too. Try them plain, but you can also add a little soy sauce.

Ingredients:

Shish Kebab skewers
2 *vegan fish filets*
1 cup yellow bell pepper, cut into 1" chunks
1 cup red bell pepper, cut into 1" chunks
1/2 zucchini, cut into 1/2" slices

1 cup pineapple, cut into 1" chunks
1/2 red onion, cut into chunks
1 lemon, juiced
Salt and pepper, to taste

Method:

1) Soak the skewers in hot water for 2 hours.
2) Assemble all vegetables in patterns along skewers. Squeeze half the lemon over finished skewers. Grill over a BBQ until cooked and slightly charred.
3) Cut the filets into 2" cubes.
4) In a serving bowl, combine the vegetables and filets. Finish with other half of lemon.

VEGAN TUNA TAPAS

Turn these tapas into extraordinary crowd- pleasers when grilled over mesquite wood chips and served with a cold beer.

Ingredients:

6-8 mini bell peppers
1 1/2 cups *vegan tuna*
1 avocado, sliced
1Tbsp sesame seeds

2 Tbsp fresh sage, chopped
2/3 cups tomatoes, chopped
Mesquite wood chips, optional

Method:

1) Squeeze out as much liquid from the vegan tuna as possible, using cheesecloth or pushing against a sieve.
2) In a small bowl, mix together tuna, avocado, seeds, sage, and tomatoes.
3) Stuff each of the bell peppers with the tuna mixture.
4) At this point, grill if doing so.

The fate of animals is of greater importance to me than the fear of appearing ridiculous; it is indissolubly connected with the fate of men.
- Émile Zola

EGGPLANT VEGAN CRAB CANAPES

The secret to crunchy eggplant chips is a slow dehydration.

Ingredients:

2 cups *vegan crab*
3/4 cup scallions
1/4 cup chives
Salt, to taste
1 1/3 Tbsp lemon juice

2 Tbsp curry
2 Tbsp tarragon
3/4 cups cucumber
1 Eggplant

Method:

1) Preheat oven to 200 degrees F.
   Cut the eggplant into rounds 1/4" thick. Bake the rounds on an ungreased cookie sheet for 2 hours to dehydrate.
2) In a large bowl, combine the crab, scallions, chives, cheese, curry powder, salt, lemon juice, curry, tarragon, cucumber. Mix well.
3) Spoon a small amount of the crabmeat mixture onto each eggplant round.

VEGAN SHRIMP COCKTAIL

This cocktail isn't just for fancy parties! The sauce also makes an excellent topping for vegan hot dogs!

Ingredients:

Vegan shrimp
2 Tbsp lemon juice
1 Tbsp worchestire sauce

1 tsp celery salt
 2 Tbsp horseradish
2 cups tomato paste
2 Tbsp brown sugar

Method:

1) In a bowl mix together all the sauce ingredients (liquids and spices), thinning with water if necessary.
2) Refrigerate 1 hour.
3) Serve with vegan shrimp.

The Animals of the planet are in desperate peril. Without free animal life I believe we will lose the spiritual equivalent of oxygen.
- Alice Walker

MAINS

BEER BATTERED VEGAN FISH

To get a fuller taste, cook the filet rice in beer instead of water! Serve with chips and vinegar or vegan tartar sauce.

Ingredients:

4 small *vegan fish filets*
½ cup dark beer
2 cups flour
Coconut oil, for frying

1 Tbsp sugar
Salt, to taste
Parsley, for garnish

Method:

1) In a skillet, melt 3 Tbsp oil over medium heat.
2) Mix the beer and flour together, adding salt to taste. If necessary, use more flour. Knead the dough for 3 minutes until soft and well combined.
3) On a floured work surface, roll out the beer dough to ¼" thickness.
4) Cut the dough into 4 strips, and cover each of the filets. Crimp the sides and corners.
5) Carefully place the 4 covered strips into the oil, and cook each side about 2-3 minutes or until golden brown.

If you have men who will exclude any of God's creatures from
the shelter of compassion and pity, you will have men who
will deal likewise with their fellow men.
- St. Francis of Assisi

VEGAN FISH au GRATIN

Spice up your potato gratin with this beautiful dish by adding vegan parmesan cheese. It's sure to please your family!

Ingredients:

4 red potatoes, thinly sliced
2 Tbsp coconut oil
½ white onion, diced
3 garlic cloves, minced
1 cup vegetable broth
1 cup cheddar flavored soy cheese
½ cup cauliflower, steamed
½ tsp paprika

1 cup coconut milk
½ cup bread crumbs
2 Tbsp flour
¼ tsp dry mustard
½ tsp nutmeg
1 cup *vegan shrimp*, chopped
vegan parmesan cheese

Method:

1) Preheat the oven to 350°F.
2) In a pot, boil the potatoes until al dente, then immediately blanch in cold water.
3) Drain and layer in a "fan" pattern in a shallow baking dish.
4) In a large pot, cook the onion and garlic until fragrant. Add the flour, stirring constantly until dissolved.
5) Add the bread crumbs.
6) Add the broth, cheese, cauliflower, milk, mustard, nutmeg, and paprika. Simmer for 3-5 minutes.
7) Pour the mixture over the potatoes. Add the shrimp Sprinkle with parmesan cheese.
8) Bake 25 minutes, or until golden.

VEGAN SHRIMP SCAMPI

When you're craving an evening summer dish, try this pasta sauce over angel hair. Serve with a rustic country loaf of bread and dine *al fresco.*

Ingredients:

2 cups *vegan shrimp*, chopped
2 Tbsp vegan butter
2 Tbsp olive oil
4 garlic cloves, minced
2 shallots, minced
Salt, to taste
1 tsp cayenne pepper
¼ cup dry vermouth

¼ cup brandy
½ cup parsley, chopped
1 tsp fresh oregano, chopped
Black pepper, to taste
½ tsp lemon zest
2 Tbsp lemon juice
1 lb. angel hair pasta, cooked and drained

Method:

1) In a skillet, melt the butter and oil over medium heat.
2) Stir in the garlic, shallots, and pepper. Sautee for 2 minutes, or until golden.
3) Add the shrimp.
4) Add the wine and brandy. Boil for 3-5 minutes, or until liquid has disappeared.
5) Remove shrimp and add parsley, oregano, black pepper, zest, and lemon juice.

"I try to live what I consider a "poetic existence." That means I take responsibility for the air I breathe and the space I take up. I try to be immediate, to be totally present for all my work."
– Maya Angelou

ITALIAN CHRISTMAS VEGAN FISH

Try the spin on this traditional favorite of grilled *Branzino* filet any time of the year. Add more culture by serving with a plate of orange slices, garlic, and parsley.

Ingredients:

2 *vegan fish filets*
2 Tbsp shallot, minced
1 tsp dried mustard
1 tsp salt
3 Tbsp white wine vinegar

1 garlic clove, minced
1 Tbsp fresh rosemary, chopped
½ cup pistachios, shelled and roasted
1/2 cup olive oil

Method:

1) In a food processor, blend the shallot, mustard, salt, vinegar, garlic, rosemary, and pistachios.
2) Slowly drizzle in the olive oil and blend until well incorporated.
3) Pour over the warm fish filet.

THAI NOODLES with VEGAN COD

This original dish served cod, but we'll be using our vegan fish filet to stand in with the appropriate spices.

Ingredients:

2 *vegan fish filets*
2 Tbsp coconut oil
½ cup scallions
2-3 cloves garlic
1 Thai pepper, chopped
½ cup green beans

1 can baby corn, split lengthwise
1 cup collard greens
2 tsp coriander
3 Tbsp maple syrup
Rice noodles, cooked

Method:

1) In a skillet, heat the oil and add the scallions and garlic over medium heat. Sautee until fragrant.
2) Add the pepper, green beans, corn, and collards. Cook until the beans are bright green.
3) Add the coriander and maple syrup. Stir until all the vegetables are coated.
4) Cover the skillet and cook on low heat for 5 minutes, or until collards are wilted and bright.
5) Serve hot over noodles.

Animals are reliable, many full of love, true in their affections, predictable in their actions, grateful and loyal. Difficult standards for people to live up to.
- Alfred A. Montapert

VEGAN CAJUN BOIL

"Do the Southern folk proud" with this comforting stew-like dish. We've substituted nut shells for the seafood shells for texture, but feel free to omit.

Ingredients:

1 ½- 2 gallons water
1 Tbsp black pepper
1 Tbsp oregano
1 Tbsp coriander
2 Tbsp cloves, ground
1 ½ Tbsp allspice, ground
2 Tbsp paprika
2 Tbsp garlic powder
3 Tbsp cayenne pepper, ground
2 Tbsp dry mustard
1 Tbsp dill, dried

salt
1 Tbsp thyme
1 tsp oregano
4 bay leaves
1 red onion, chopped
4 red potatoes, cubed
2 ears of corn, cut into 4" cobs and roasted
1 cup large nut shells (almond, walnut, brazilian)
*Vegan shrimp**

Method:

1) In a large pot, add water and all spices. Bring to a boil.
2) Into the pot add the red onions, potatoes, and shells. Cook ½ hour on a low simmer.
3) Add your "shrimp" dough and cook until floating.
4) Add your corn cobs and cook 5 minutes.
5) Serve immediately.

*NOTE: Prepare the vegan shrimp dough per the recipe, and slice the shrimp strips. However, do not cook or fry. We will be cooking the vegan shrimp in Cajun spiced water for this recipe.

VEGAN FISH TACOS

Serve these tacos as a large burrito, or small street tacos depending on the tortilla size. Enjoy with a *cervesa* after a hard day's work.

Ingredients:

For fish:
1 cup Sushi rice, cooked
1/3 cup cauliflower, steamed
½ cup v*egan salmon spread*
Whole wheat bread*
Coconut oil

For tacos:
1 large tortilla or 4 small tortillas

2/3 cup tomato, chopped
¾ cup romaine lettuce, chopped
½ white onion, minced

For dressing:
1 cup cilantro
½ cup vegan sour cream
1 Jalapeño, diced

Method:

1) *To make the fish:* In a skillet, melt 5 Tbsp coconut oil. In a bowl, combine the rice, cauliflower, and salmon. Mix well. Cut the crusts off your bread. In the center of each bread square, spoon the mixture in a vertical strip, about 1" wide. Fold the other sides up and pinch along the ridge. You should have a thin, long triangle. Repeat with remaining slices until mixture is used. Fry the sticks in oil, rotating to cook all sides. Fry about 3 minutes per side, or until golden.
2) *To make the tacos:* Assemble your tacos with the remaining ingredients.
3) *To make the dressing*: In a food processor, combine the cilantro, sour cream, and jalapeno.
4) Serve the dressing on top of tacos, and enjoy!

*NOTE: Most bread should be Vegan, as basic bread dough is made from flour, water, salt, and yeast. But just in case, read your ingredients!

VEGAN TUNA CASSEROLE

Make this dish ahead and warm in the oven for a quick weekday dinner. Serve plain or with catsup.

Ingredients:

2 cups *vegan tuna*
3 cups vegan fusilli pasta, cooked and drained
1 white onion, diced
1 cup celery, chopped

3 cloves garlic, minced
Salt and pepper, to taste
1 cup cheddar flavored soy cheese

Method:

1) Preheat the oven to 350°F.
2) In a large bowl, combine the tuna, pasta, white onion, celery, garlic, salt, and pepper.
3) Pour into a 9x13 baking dish. Cover the mixture with vegan cheddar cheese.
4) Cook the casserole for 20 minutes, or until the cheese is melted and golden.
5) Let cool 10 minutes. Serve.

I am in favor of animal rights as well as human rights.
That is the way of a whole human being.
-Abraham Lincoln

BLACKENED GRILLED VEGAN SALMON

The key to this dish is adding the Vegan Salmon spread when making the fish filets. Serve over black or white rice.

Ingredients:

4 *vegan fish filets**
2 cups Vegan Vegan Salmon spread
2 Tbsp Fresh cracked black pepper
1 Tbsp Lemon zest
2 tsp Paprika

1 Tbsp cayenne pepper, ground
1 Tbsp onion Powder
Salt, to taste
Coconut Oil

Method:

1) Preheat a griddle or grill. Brush with coconut oil .
2) In an empty casserole dish, combine the pepper, zest, paprika, cayenne, onion powder, and salt.
3) Slightly wet the filet skins with water then lay the filets in the spice mixture. Flip the filets to coat both sides.
4) Grill the filets for 2-4 minutes on each side, or until crispy.
5) Serve immediately.

   * NOTE: When making the vegan fish filets, add 2 cups of salmon mixture to the cooked rice and use in the nori sheets. Steam as usual.

VEGAN TILAPIA with MANGO SALSA

The salsa keeps well, so feel free to make it ahead and store in the refrigerator.

Ingredients:

2 *vegan fish filets*

1 cup coconut water

For the sauce:
1 tsp onion powder
1 cup orange juice
2 Tbsp maple syrup
1 tsp ginger, ground
1 tsp cayenne pepper, ground
Black pepper, to taste

For the salsa:
1 cup mango, cubed
1 cup avocado, cubed
1 tsp shallot, minced

Method:

1) *To make the sauce:* In a saucepan, combine the onion powder, juice, syrup, ginger, cayenne, black pepper, and coconut water over medium heat. Simmer about 20 minutes, or until liquid is thicker and reduced in half.
2) *To make the salsa:* In a bowl, combine the mango, avocado, and shallot.
3) Serve the fish filets with the salsa, drizzling the sauce over everything.

The worst sin towards our fellow creatures is not to hate them, but to be indifferent to them. That's the essence of inhumanity.
- George Bernard Shaw

ALMOND CRUSTED- VEGAN HALIBUT with CRANBERRIES

This dish is especially tasty around Christmas when cranberries are abundant. If you have extra berries in the package, make a garland with popcorn.

Ingredients:

2 *vegan fish filets*
3 Tbsp flax seed
¼ cup warm water
Vegan butter
½ cup almond meal

For the sauce:
1 cup cranberries
½ tsp thyme
½ tsp lemon zest
2 Tbsp maple syrup
½ tsp fresh nutmeg, grated

Method:

1) In a bowl, combine the flax seed and water. Let sit for 5 minutes.
2) In a skillet, melt the butter over medium heat.
3) On a plate, pour out the almond meal.
4) Wipe the fish filets with the flax seed liquid then batter in the almond meal.
5) Fry immediately, about 3-5 minutes per side, or until crispy.
6) *To make the sauce:* In a saucepan, combine all the ingredients. Simmer, covered, for 10-15 minutes or until all the cranberries are popped and the liquid is thick.
7) Serve the filets with the sauce warm or chilled.

BAKED VEGAN CRAB ENCHILADAS

This Mexican favorite was traditionally make with chicken, but crab is a worthy substitute. Consider freezing the unbaked dish. When you're ready to eat, thaw the dish and bake as usual to enjoy with the family!

Ingredients:

Coconut oil
1 ½ cups *vegan crab*
1 cup scallions
½ cup tomato paste
½ cup vegan cream cheese
2 cups spinach
3 cloves garlic, minced

1 cup brown rice, cooked
paprika
1 can black beans, drained
Salt and pepper, to taste
8-10 tortillas
1 can green enchilada sauce
1 cup vegan cheese, shredded.

Method:

1) Preheat the oven to 400°F.
2) Grease a 9x13 glass dish with oil.
3) In a large bowl combine the cram, scallions, tomato paste, cream cheese, spinach, garlic, rice, paprika, beans, salt, and pepper. Mix well.
4) Fill a tortilla with 1/3 cup crab mixture, then roll and place in the dish. Repeat until all the crab mixture is used.
5) Pout the enchilada sauce over all the rolls. Top with cheese.
6) Bake 20-25 minutes, or until the cheese is melted and golden.

VEGAN SALMON RAVIOLIS

You don't need a pasta maker for this Italian dish. A wise surface and a rolling pin work just as well.

Ingredients:

1 cup *vegan salmon spread*
½ cup chives
1 cup kale, chopped and wilted
1 cup flour
¼ cup water

3 Tbsp flax meal
Lemon juice, to garnish
Capers, to garnish
Vegan parmesan cheese, to garnish

Method:

1) Bring a large pot of water to a boil.
2) In a bowl mix the spread, chives, and kale.
3) In another bowl mix the flour, water, and flax meal. Add more water if needed. Knead for 3-5 minutes. Let dough rest for 10 minutes.
4) Roll the dough on a floured surface to ½" thick. Cut into 2" squares.
5) Onto half the squares, spoon 1 tsp of the salmon mixture. Place the remaining squares over the mixture and crimp edges closed with a fork.
6) Carefully drop the raviolis into the boiling water, cooking 5-10 minutes, or until they float.
7) Remove and serve immediately with lemon juice, capers, and cheese sprinkled over the top.

CURRIED VEGAN FISH

Based on a Jamaican recipe, this fish can easily be turned into a soup with added broth. Just cut the filets into chunks and serve in a bowl.

Ingredients:

2 *vegan fish filets*
3 Tbsp coconut oil
2 Tbsp curry
½ tsp cayenne pepper, ground
½ yellow onion, chopped
1 cup green bell pepper, diced

3 cloved garlic, minced
1 scotch bonnet chile, minced
1 tsp fresh thyme, chopped
1 cup broccoli
1 can coconut milk
Scallions, to garnish

Method:

1) Melt the coconut oil in a large skillet over medium heat.
2) Add the curry, cayenne, onion, bell pepper, garlic, chile, thyme, and broccoli and cook until fragrant with soft onions, about 5 minutes.
3) Add the coconut milk and simmer 10 minutes.
4) Pour the sauce over the fish, and garnish with scallions cut on the diagonal.
5) Serve immediately.

"The trouble with always trying to preserve the health of the body
is that it is so difficult to do without destroying the health of the mind."
- G.K. Chesterton

BAKEN PARMESAN VEGAN TROUT

While there are several vegan parmesan recipes out there, we've found the cashew ones are very stable. Store extra "parm" in the fridge in a mason or other covered jar.

Ingredients:

2 *vegan fish filets*
Coconut oil
2 Tbsp basil, dried
1 tsp black pepper
1 Tbsp lemon zest

¼ cup lemon juice
½ cups bread crumbs
1 cup vegan parmesan cheese
Marinara sauce
1 eggplant, sliced and grilled

Method:

1) Preheat the oven to 350°F.
2) Grease a 9x13 glass dish with coconut oil.
3) In a shallow dish, combine the basil, pepper, lemon zest, bread crumbs, and ½ cup cheese.
4) Brush the filets with the lemon juice, then coat in the breadcrumb mixture. Place into the baking dish. Bake uncovered for 10-15 minutes, or until cheese is golden.
5) Remove from oven and pour over marinara sauce and top with remaining cheese.
6) Return to the oven and back another 10 minutes.

SUSHI

BLACK RICE TERIYAKI

Black rice gives this sushi an evening elegance. Dip the rolls in traditional wasabi or leave plain!

Ingredients:

Filling:
1 package tofu
2 parsnips, diced and boiled
3 garlic cloves, chopped
3 Tbsp tamari
2 Tbsp olive oil
2 tsp Spanish Smoked Paprika
1/2 cucumber

1 avocado, mashed
1 cup black rice, cooked
Nori sheets

Glue:
2 Tbsp Arrowroot Powder
2 Tbsp warm water

Method:

1) Cut the tofu, parsnips, cucumber into long strips.
2) Sautee strips in tamari, paprika, and oil.
3) *To assemble the sushi*: Lay a nori sheet onto a cutting board. Brush the sheet with the glue. Spread avocado onto the bottom half of the sheet. Spread the rice on top. Lay down the vegetables. Roll up and seal the edge with glue, like an envelope. Your ends should be exposed.
4) Repeat the process with remaining nori sheets until the avocado, rice and vegetables are used.
5) Slice into rounds, using a sharp serrated knife.

CALIFORNIA GARDEN ROLE

Try this vegan twist on a classic favorite. Add some *Vegan Salmon spread* for a fishy bite, and dip the rolls in wasabi with soy sauce.

Ingredients:

1 cup Sushi rice, cooked
4 pieces nori seaweed
1 cup avocado, mashed
1 Tbsp lemon juice
1 package tofu
1 cucumber, sliced into matchsticks
2 celery stalks, sliced into matchsticks
3 steamed carrots, sliced into matchsticks

½ yellow bell pepper, sliced into matchsticks

Glue:
2 Tbsp Arrowroot Powder
2 Tbsp warm water

Method:
1) Combine the avocado and lemon juice.
2) Carefully cut the tofu into matchsticks.
3) *To assemble the sushi*: Lay a nori sheet onto a cutting board. Brush the sheet with the glue. Spread the avocado mixture on the bottom half of the sheet. Spread the rice on top. Lay tofu and vegetables across rice. Roll up and seal the edge with glue, like an envelope. Your ends should be exposed.
4) Repeat the process with remaining nori sheets until the ingredients are used.
5) Slice into rounds, using a sharp serrated knife.

WHOLE GRAINS and SEEDS

Sprout these grains and seeds for an even healthier option. Serve with any dipping sauce.

Ingredients:

1/2 cup quinoa rice, uncooked
2 cups filtered water
3 Tbsp flax meal
4 pieces nori seaweed
1 cup cauliflower, steamed
3 Tbsp sunflower seeds
1 cucumber, sliced into matchsticks
1 shitake mushroom, sliced

3 Tbsp nama shoyu
1/4 cup mung bean sprouts

Glue:
2 Tbsp Arrowroot Powder
2 Tbsp warm water

Method:

1) In a bowl, marinate the mushrooms in nama shoyu.
2) In a pot, combine quinoa, water, and flax meal. Bring to a boil, then simmer covered for about 15-25 minutes. Fluff and let cool.
3) In a food processor, combine cauliflower and sunflower seeds. Blend until smooth a paste forms.
4) *To assemble the sushi*: Lay a nori sheet onto a cutting board. Brush the sheet with the glue. Spread the cauliflower paste over the bottom half of the sheet. Spoon the quinoa mixture onto the paste, pressing firmly. Lay vegetables across the quinoa. Roll up and seal the edge with glue, like an envelope. Your ends should be exposed.
5) Repeat the process with remaining nori sheets until the ingredients are used.
6) Slice into rounds, using a sharp serrated knife.

SPICY BRUSSELS POUCH

Vegan Tuna makes this recipe similar to a "Spicy Tuna Roll," but adding the brussel sprouts gives your mouth time to recover between bites. Dip in homemade teriyaki sauce to finish your masterpiece.

Ingredients:

Vegan tuna
Yuba*
½ cup brussel sprouts, steamed
Spicy sesame oil
2 tsp. rice vinegar
1 avocado, sliced
4 slices red bell pepper
Sushi rice, cooked

Teriyaki Sauce:
3 Tbsp tamari
2 Tbsp maple syrup
1 Tbsp pineapple juice
1/2 tsp garlic powder
1/4 tsp ground ginger
2 tsp onion powder
1 Tbsp catsup

Method:

1) In a bowl, mash the brussel sprouts.
2) In another bowl combine tuna, oil, and vinegar.
3) Add avocado, bell pepper, and brussel sprouts.
4) Stuff each tofu packet with the tuna and vegetable mixture.
5) *To make the sauce*: Mix all the ingredients.

   NOTE: See note about yuba in the Vegan Fish Filet recipe.

PARSLEY CURRIED TEMPEH

Sushi goes international with this Mediterranean touch to a traditionally Indian spice. Skip the wasabi, and opt for vegan mayonnaise with lemon juice.

Ingredients:

Sushi rice, cooked
4 pieces nori seaweed
1 packet tempeh, cut into ¼" cubes
¼ tsp coconut oil
1/3 cup shallot
1 tsp fresh ginger, grated
2 cloves garlic, minced
¼ tsp Dijon mustard
½ tsp cumin

1 ½ tsp curry powder
1/8 tsp cayenne, dried
3 Tbsp parsley, minced
½ cup light coconut milk
Salt to taste

Glue:
2 Tbsp Arrowroot Powder
2 Tbsp warm water

Method:

1) In a skillet over medium heat add the oil and shallots, cooking until fragrant.
2) Add the ginger, garlic, mustard, and cumin. Stir and cook until fragrant.
3) Add the curry, cayenne, tempeh, and parsley.
4) Add the coconut milk and salt. Cook, until the liquid is mostly absorbed, stirring frequently.* Let the mixture cool.
5) *To assemble the sushi*: Lay a nori sheet onto a cutting board. Brush the sheet with the glue. Spoon the tempeh mixture over the bottom half of the sheet. Spread the rice on top. Roll up and seal the edge with glue, like an envelope. Your ends should be exposed.
6) Repeat the process with remaining nori sheets until the ingredients are used.
7) Slice into rounds, using a sharp serrated knife.

*NOTE: Do not overcook this mixture, or the sauce will separate and become unusable.

FOR KIDS

TUNA SANDWICH

Watch kids eat this sandwich with vigor. They will forget it's not real fish!

Ingredients:

½ cup *vegan tuna*
2 slices whole wheat bread
3 slices cucumber
1 romaine lettuce leaf
1 tsp Dijon mustard

Method:

1) Spread the bread slices with the mustard.
2) Add the tuna on one side of the sandwich.
3) Layer the cucumbers on top of the tuna.
4) Add the lettuce over the cucumbers.
5) Finish with the plain slice of bread
6) Depending on the age of your child (or adult), cut the bread into desired shapes using cookie cutters.

FISH STICKS

These are best eaten fresh, dipped in catsup or vegan tartar sauce!

Ingredients:

1 cup Sushi rice, cooked
1/3 cup cauliflower, steamed
½ cup vegan salmon spread

Whole wheat bread*
Coconut oil

Method:

1) In a skillet, melt 5 Tbsp coconut oil.
2) In a bowl, combine the rice, cauliflower, and salmon. Mix well.
3) Cut the crusts off your bread.
4) *To make the sticks:* In the center of each bread square, spoon the mixture in a vertical strip, about 1" wide. Fold the other sides up and pinch along the ridge. You should have a thin, long triangle. Repeat with remaining slices until mixture is used.
5) Fry the sticks in oil, rotating to cook all sides. Fry about 3 minutes per side, or until golden.

*NOTE: Most bread should be Vegan, as basic bread dough is made from flour, water, salt, and yeast. But just in case, read your ingredients!

"There are two freedoms; The false, where man is free to do what he likes; The true, where man is free to do what he ought."
– Charles Kingsley

VEGAN BBQ FRITTERS

Homemade Barbeque sauce is delicious and nutritious, without added preservatives and chemicals like high-fructose corn syrup.

Ingredients:

For the fritters:
4 cups water
1 cup *vegan crab*
½ cup cauliflower, cooked and drained
½ cup breadcrumbs
2 Tbsp parsley
Salt and pepper, to taste
3 Tbsp flax meal
Coconut oil, for frying

For BBQ sauce:
2 tablespoons olive oil
1 small yellow onion, chopped
1 Tbsp tomato paste
2 Tbsp white wine vinegar
2 Tbsp brown sugar
1 tsp mustard powder
2 Tbsp Worcestershire sauce
Water, to thin

Method:

1) In a large pot, bring water to a boil.
2) Squeeze as much liquid from the crab as possible, either in cheesecloth or against a sieve. Do the same to the cauliflower.
3) In a large bowl, mix the crab meat, cauliflower, bread crumbs, parsley, salt, pepper, and flaxmeal. Let sit 10 minutes.
4) In a large skillet, melt 4 Tbsp coconut oil over medium high heat. Carefully drop spoonfuls of the cram mixture into the skillet and fry on all sides, about 3-5 minutes until golden.
5) *To make the sauce*: Heat the oil in a skillet over medium heat. Add the onions and fry for 3-4 minutes, until translucent. Stir in the tomato paste.* Add the rest of the ingredients. Bring the mixture to the boil and simmer for 10-15 minutes. Blend in a food processor or blender, adding water to thin to desired consistency.

   *NOTE: Add the tomato paste separately to avoid forming red chunks with the other ingredients.

DRESSINGS and SAUCES

CEASAR DRESSING

Ancient Romans would savor this dressing as much in history as in modern day. Serve with salads, wraps, or as a dip for vegetables.

Ingredients:

2 Tbsp Dijon mustard
2 Tbsp nutritional yeast flakes
2 Tbsp almond butter
3 garlic cloves, minced
2 Tbsp lemon juice
½ Tbsp soy sauce
1 Tbsp olive oil

1/4 tsp ground pepper
1 ½ tsp mild miso
½ tsp dill, dried
Kelp flakes, to taste
Pinch of Stevia
Filtered water, to thin

Method:

1) In a food processor blend together the mustard, yeast flakes, butter, and garlic.
2) In a bowl, combine the lemon juice, soy sauce, olive oil, and miso.
3) Add the liquids to the mustard mixture while processor is on, drizzling in slowly.
4) Add pepper, kelp flakes, and stevia, continuing to blend.
5) Add water if mixture is too thick.
6) Refrigerate 1 hour in a mason jar. Shake well before serving.

"As human beings, we are endowed with freedom of choice, and we cannot shuffle off our responsibility upon the shoulders of God or nature. We must shoulder it ourselves. It is our responsibility."
– Arnold Toynbee

FISH SAUCE

Use this fish sauce for a direct substitute in pescatarian dishes, using a 1:1 ratio. Keep in a sealed jar for 1-2 weeks.

Ingredients:

1 1/2 cups wakame
6 cups water
6 cloves garlic

1 Tbsp peppercorns
1 cup nama shoyu
3 Tbsp pineapple juice
1 Tbsp mild miso

Method:

1) Crush the garlic; do not peel.
2) In a large saucepan, combine the wakame, garlic, peppercorns and water and bring to a boil.
3) Lower heat and simmer for 20 minutes.
4) Strain the contents, and return the liquid to the pot.
5) Add nama shoyu and juice, and return to a boil.
6) Cook until mixture is reduced and very salty.
7) Remove from heat and stir in miso.

SPICY ORANGE MISO SAUCE

Though this sauce is wonderful in sushi fillings, it shines atop plain, steamed vegan fish filets with steamed peas.

Ingredients:

1 tsp orange zest
1 cup orange juice
1 Tbsp miso
1 Tbsp ginger, grated

2 tsp rice wine vinegar
2 tsp spicy sesame oil
1 cup vegetable stock
¼ tsp cayenne pepper

Method:

1) In a small saucepan combine all the ingredients. Whisk well until thoroughly blended.
2) Bring to a boil and simmer on medium heat until reduced in half.
3) Serve immediately, or store in the refrigerator.

"You are responsible, forever, for what you have tamed.
You are responsible for your rose."
- Antoine de Saint-Exupery

LIST of INGREDIENTS

Allspice	Cucumber
Almond Butter	Cumin
Almond Meal	Curry
Apples	Dark Beer
Arrowroot Powder	Dill, fresh and dried
Avocado	Eggplant
Bagels	Flax meal
Basil, dried	Flour
Bay Leaves	Garlic; fresh and powder
Bell Pepper; red, green, orange	Ginger, ground and fresh
Black Beans	Gluten Flour
Black Pepper	Grape Tomatoes
Brandy	Green Beans
Bread Crumbs	Green Enchilada Sauce
Bread; whole wheat, sourdough	Horseradish
Broccoli	Jalapeno
Brown Sugar	Kale
Brussel Sprouts	Kelp Granules
Capers	Lemon, zest and juice
Carrots	Lemongrass
Catsup	Lettuce, romaine
Cauliflower	Lime, zest and juice
Cayenne Pepper	Mango
Celery Salt	Maple Syrup
Celery	Marinara Sauce
Chickpea Flour	Mesquite Wood Chips
Chickpeas	Miso Paste
Chili Powder	Mung Bean Sprouts
Chives, fresh	Mushrooms; crimini, shitake
Cilantro	Mustard; yellow, Dijon, dry
Cloves	Nama Shoyu
Coconut Milk	Nori Sheets
Coconut Oil	Nut Shells; almond, walnut, brazilian
Coconut Water	Nutmeg, freshly grated
Collard Greens	Nutritional Yeast
Coriander	Olive Oil
Corn; ears, canned baby	Onion Powder
Cranberries	Onion; yellow, white, red

Orange; zest and juice

Oregano, fresh and dried

Paprika

Parsley, fresh and dried

Pasta; angel hair, fusilli

Peanut Oil

Pesto

Pine Nuts

Pineapple; fruit, juice

Pistachios

Potatoes; golden, red

Quinoa

Rice Noodles

Rice Vinegar

Rice Wine Vinegar

Rice; black, white Sushi, brown

Rosemary, fresh

Sage, fresh

Salt

Scotch Bonnet Chili

Seaweed, dulse and wakame

Serrano Chili

Sesame Oil

Sesame Seeds

Shallots

Sherry

Shish kebab skewers

Slivered Almonds

Smoked Tofu

Soy Cheese, cheddar flavored

Spinach

Spanish Smoked Paprika

Stevia

Sunflower Seeds

Sweet Potato Puree

Sweet Potatoes

Sweet Relish

Tahini

Tamari

Tarragon, dried or fresh

Tempeh

Thai Pepper

Thyme, dried and fresh

Tofu

Tomato Paste

Tomatoes

Tortillas

Turmeric

Vegan Butter

Vegan Cheese

Vegan Cream Cheese

Vegan Croutons

Vegan Mayonnaise

Vegan Parmesan Cheese

Vegan Pasta

Vegan Pastry Crust

Vegan Sour Cream

Vegetable Broth

Vegetarian Bouillon Powder

Vermouth, dry

Walnuts

Water

Watercress

White Sugar

White Wine Vinegar

White Wine, dry

Whole Wheat Bread

Wonton Wrappers

Worchestire Sauce

Yuba

Zucchini

INDEX, alphabetical

CONCLUSION

We hope you've enjoyed this book and become more comfortable in the kitchen. Vegan cooking might sometimes require creativity, since you are new to it but I encourage you to be patience and start exploring! I praise the choice to cook your own food, whether or not it stems from social awareness.

You've conquered soups and sauces, main courses, homemade dressings, and even food for the kids. Well done! Don't stop there… continue to experiment with ingredients to find favorites for your lifestyle.

Bon appétit!

Bonus: Get Lots Of Valuable Information & A FREE Copy Of:

The 3 "Health" Foods You Need To Stop Eating!

Recommended Books

Below you'll find some of my other popular books that are popular on Amazon and Kindle as well. Simply click on the links below to check them out. Alternatively, you can visit my author page on Amazon to see other work done by me.

Everything That Used To Have Cheese, Is Now Vegan: Don't Give Up Your Favorite Recipes Only Because It Has Cheese

Raw Till 4: A Monthly Meal Plan - 90 Amazing Recipes to Keep You Healthy

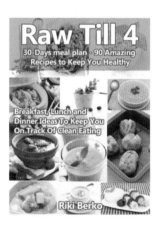

Vegan Kids Box Set: Vegan Recipes For Kids & Vegan Diet For Kids

Build Muscle on the Raw Vegan Diet: How to Gain Muscle Mass, Get   Big and Be Fit on the Raw Food Diet

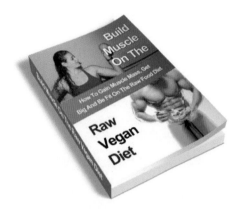

Food Addiction: How To Develop Self Discipline, Control Your Eating And Overcome Food Addiction

Anti Aging From Within: How To Look Younger And Slow Down The Aging Process Naturally and Economically

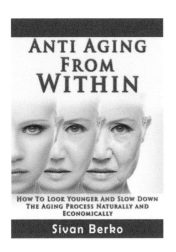

If the links do not work, for whatever reason, you can simply search for these titles on the Amazon website to find them.

Printed in Great Britain
by Amazon

76605099R00040